MW01264913

ISBN: 9781314669480

Published by:
HardPress Publishing
8345 NW 66TH ST #2561
MIAMI FL 33166-2626

Email: info@hardpress.net
Web: http://www.hardpress.net

THE FACE OF PRAGUE

L'IMAGE DE PRAGUE

———

ARTIA

THE FACE OF PRAGUE

L'IMAGE DE PRAGUE

Photographs by M. Kučera

Designed and produced by Artia • Prague

Printed in Czechoslovakia

I T IS HARD, indeed, to find the right words for a preface to a pictorial poem about Prague which would give foreigners at least some idea of its true appearance.

The ancient seat of the Bohemian kings, an international centre of the art world, the cradle of the Hussite movement, the conservatoire of Europe... An immortal heart at the cross-roads of history, whose pulse has often stimulated world events in turbulent times.

The golden, hundred-towered city on the Vltava...

Praised a thousand times in such terms throughout the ages by artists in words, colour and sound, beloved and remembered by all who have ever enjoyed the hospitality of its walls...

Wherein lies that magic charm which ruffles the calm of observation into admiring emotion in the mind of the traveller, who – though he may have seen the loveliest cities in the world – seeing Prague once, is forever enchanted?

Is it the overwhelming richness of the impressions received from the pictures which spring to mind and are born of the tempestuous political and artistic seethings of long centuries?

Or is it those thousands of different faces with which Prague forever succeeds in charming one anew despite the destructive ravages of time, and which can match those of any city of the modern world?

In truth, thousands of faces of great beauty, glowing with the radiance of a precious stone, burnished by the centuries... How many of them have witnessed the growth and development of this city, in whose lap lies a treasury of precious architectural and artistic gems! For centuries the Vltava has sung the same song as it wound its way through Prague, but all the while the city itself with its ever-changing faces has been mirrored in the river's surface and it is hard to judge which of them has been the more beautiful. Yet... there is one that enchants more than the rest, though it is marked with deep furrows and the fierce stream of life has heedlessly covered it with the growth of buildings of more modern times.

It is the oldest face of the "Mother of our Towns", precious and moving as only a mother's face can be, where age has not dimmed the former grace of youth. A gracious smiling face, proud even in its calm acceptance of the now silenced romance of times gone by, and yet forever encouraging new generations with a noble desire for beauty.

Let's take a look, then, at Prague, if we want to get to know and understand her! Let's start from the hills, where history began to write its glorious and dramatic epic, let's wander down through the floral paradise of gardens, where we may yet catch an echo of the whimsical games of the shepherds in the songs and whisperings of the centuries-old trees... Let's make the silent corners of the old nobles' palaces ring with the sound of our footsteps; perhaps lose ourselves in the idyllic labyrinth of tiny passages in the Little Town quarter and savour the enchanting views and vistas which suddenly open up before our eyes...

The Face of Prague is the first book in the new Artion series. There could certainly have been no better choice than to commence the series with a book devoted to the ancient beauty of the hundred-towered city on the Vltava.

We are glad that it will carry this message of beauty far across the frontiers and bring a friendly greeting from a nation that has embodied its noblest efforts, its love, and its faith in the future and the eternal glory and joy of life on earth in the thousandfold enchantments of its capital city...

Jiří Körber

LIST OF PHOTOGRAPHS

FRONT COVER PAGE. For centuries the river Vltava has flowed under the oldest stone bridge in Prague, the Charles Bridge, whose Tower forms the entrance gate to the enchanting historical relics of the quarter known as the Little Town.

1. The old ramparts of THE VYŠEHRAD FORTRESS are a relic from the times of the ancient prophecy made by the legendary Princess Libuše, concerning the future of the town of Prague: "that its glory would one day reach the stars".

2. Not even the busy life of to-day, making them ring with the sound of happy children's laughter, can dispel from the ruins of the Vyšehrad fortress their twilight veil of ancient legends about heroes who in defence of their city acquitted themselves with bravery and honour.

3. The path leads down, as if to a carefully guarded treasury of jewels, to the infinite wealth of Prague's ancient relics lying in the broad lap of the town.

4. On the opposite bank of the Vltava, close to the Castle, a jewel of Renaissance architecture— the Belvedere royal pavilion—stands out above the luxuriant vegetation of the Royal Gardens. The pavilion dates back to the beginning of the 16th century.

5. Each year the magic of Spring in Prague weaves a new and lovely frame to the picture its people love most dearly—the view of its hundreds of spires and towers.

6. Above the gay mosaic of the garden slopes, as though uplifted by an arched wave of greenery, rises the famous STRAHOV MONASTERY, with its valuable collections of manuscripts and old books, to-day known as the Museum of National Literature.

7. From the maze of alley-ways below the Castle, these steps seem to lead to the underworld. But in reality it is only one of many paths which take us down into the heart of the Little Town.

8. This arcade in the Little Town, not far from WALLENSTEIN SQUARE, has not lost the charm of bygone days. It is only that the sound of the footsteps of workaday life has to-day taken the place of the clinking spurs of splendidly accoutred knights.

9. Through the arcades in front of the time-honoured TÝN CHURCH rings the sound of children's laughter, awakening memories of eventful moments in Prague's history, when in times of peace the Týn bells pealed in rejoicing, or sounded the alarm in moments of danger.

10. THE GOLDEN LANE of the Castle is a memorial to the bustling days of Emperor Rudolf II, when artists and scientists from many lands made Prague a meeting place. A romantic aura of legends about the misguided struggles of the alchemists seems to hang over the cottages to this very day.

11. In contrast: the picturesque surroundings of HRADČANY SQUARE, where the old patrician houses with their characteristic portals and carefully placed windows bring to mind the harmonious unity of the Renaissance.

12. Not far from the busy centre of the modern metropolis—and yet here is the peacefulness of an age when quiet steps came to a contemplative halt before the MALTESE CHURCH OF OUR LADY, at the end of the bridge.

13. Like a creeper that gently covers the scars of an ageing house, memories now weave themselves around the area of FIVE CHURCHES SQUARE; from there one can climb up to the restaurant known as "The Golden Well", which commands one of the finest views in Prague.

14. This corner of the LEDEBURG GARDEN, with its enchanting terraces, shows only a tiny portion of the treasury of old palace gardens in the area of the Little Town, where luxuriant vegetation often hides architectural gems and artistic achievements of the eighteenth century.

15. The famous Baroque master, Matthias Braun, decorated the picturesque corners of the VRTBA GARDEN with monumental sculptures; to this day it is a favourite haunt of young people.

16. Even the entrances to the old Prague gardens have their own particular charm, suggesting sunny gates opening on to a paradise of flowers, where nature's magic lightens the cares and worries of the outside world.

17. THE DEVIL'S BROOK, lapping the ancient foundations of the Little Town houses, perpetually re-creates romantic scenes from the past. The ancient mill-wheel alone is enough to give one the impression that time here has come to a stop.

18. A step further and the Vltava is singing yet another verse of its eternal song of the irresistible passage of time; but the traveller pauses a while on the banks of KAMPA ISLAND, in order to savour to the full the magic of Prague's oldest bridge, the Charles Bridge.

19. A few steps on, and we see before us the most beautiful view of all, one that has charmed

everyone who has ever set eyes on it the panorama of the royal HRADČANY CASTLE above the Vltava.

20. A walk across the medieval CHARLES BRIDGE is at the same time a review of Czech Baroque sculpture. In particular Matthias Braun and the two Brokoffs created splendid expressive works at the beginning of the eighteenth century.

21. The all-conquering power of music would seem to have affected even the stones in front of the famous RUDOLFINUM—the House of Artists. At one time temporarily the seat of Parliament, the building has now been restored to its original function. Sheltered beneath the protecting silhouette of the Hradčany, the Prague Spring International Music Festivals now ring forth there with a symphony of sound in praise of beauty and peace.

22. It is not far from the Little Town to Prague OLD TOWN, and the real heart of the city. Dim secluded stairways to-day lead one to the various art treasures now in the safe-keeping of the museums.

23. Before THE OLD TOWN HALL, proud witness of the saddest and most glorious moments of the Czech nation, the ages—the most ancient, the recent past, and the modern era of to-day—seem to meet as at a cross-roads.

24. From the Old Town Hall there is a picturesque view of THE TÝN CHURCH, dating from the fourteenth and fifteenth centuries; many times immortalized, not only on painter's canvasses but also in the glorious annals of the Hussite period of Prague's history.

25. In many parts of Prague we still come across the remains of old fortifications dating from the period when Prague was originally a walled town. In CARMELITE STREET, in the Little Town, there is a tiny ornamental house crouched between more modern buildings, built over the ruins of what was formerly one of Prague's oldest gates.

26. An inseparable part of the Hradčany panorama, dominating the whole Little Town, is the mighty CHURCH OF ST. NICOLAS, a superb work of art by Kilián Ignac Dientzenhofer—a real gem of Czech Baroque architecture.

27. An ornamental sculpture on the outer wall of St. Nicolas's Church. In the background is St. Vitus's Cathedral in Prague Castle, where the remains of the Czech kings lie buried.

28. The rich interwoven stone tracery encircling the tower of St. Vitus's Cathedral is a striking example of superb Gothic ornamentation and one of the unforgettable sights of Prague.

29. Not far away, just below the Castle, even the later masters of such crafts did not spare their imagination when ornamenting the open spaces of the Old Town, as we see from the decorations on the Renaissance fountain in "The Little Rhine".

30. To-day, as they were a hundred years ago, the windows of the dwellings in the Little Town opened wide on to the quaint squares and alleyways. For the pleasure of the public, some former owner decorated the portals and cornices with sculptural decoration that is a delight to the eye.

31. The wealth of forms and the fantasy of the Baroque style gave burghers plenty of scope in decorating their gables with the individual charm of their personal emblems.

32. In contrast, as though shutting itself off strictly from all secular life and wishing to emphasize its power by making a grand impression, the Church thrust up the cold masonry of its church towers to ever greater heights. To this day the oldest bell in Prague rings from the tower of the Dominican Church of ST. GILES in Huss Street.

33. The nobility, though professing support for the ideals of the Renaissance during the sixteenth century, likewise shut themselves off from the common life of the world by building luxurious palaces. THE SCHWARZENBERG PALACE, standing on the ramp of Hradčany Castle, dates from this time; it is richly ornamented in graffito.

34. The stairways, so typical of the old quarter of the town, often lead the traveller out of the close labyrinth of alley-ways to unexpected vantage points. One of the most romantic ways of reaching Prague Castle is to walk up THE CASTLE STEPS from Thun Street.

35. Like a curious child, a ray of sunlight for a moment penetrates the dimness of SASKÁ STREET behind the Charles Bridge, as if to convince itself that life has not altogether disappeared from the oldest districts.

36. From the space in front of the outer courtyard of Prague Castle we are offered an enchanting view of the old tiled roofs of Little Town in the foggy haze of dawn, or under the golden veil of twilight.

37. From the church of Our Lady in the Chains we look out on to historic Maltese Square and the Baroque statue of St. John the Baptist, which once formed the centre of a fountain.

38. Not even the harsh critical glare of artificial light can disturb the centuries-old beauty of THE LITTLE TOWN BRIDGE TOWERS. On the contrary, against

the pitch dark of the night these architectural gems of former centuries are more impressive than ever.

39. THE BLACK TOWER, a rare Romanesque relic, dates from the first stone fortification of Prague Castle in the twelfth century, and has preserved its charm in spite of the destruction caused by several fires.

40. And now, for the last time, another picture that is certain to be remembered by all who have once seen it: night is falling over Charles Bridge, enveloping the face of Prague in a starry veil of dreams.

BACK COVER PAGE. The John Huss memorial, in front of the Týn Church, guards the memory and glory of this Hussite city, where beauty is inextricably linked with the noble ideals of the people, who are always ready to welcome all who come with good intentions.

Jiří Körber

E CRIRE la préface de cette épopée en prose et en images, destinée à mieux faire connaître Prague aux étrangers, est en vérité une tâche ardue. Les mots sont, à cet usage, bien pauvres et bien imparfaits.

Prague… ancienne résidence des rois de Bohême, point de ralliement international du monde artistique, berceau du mouvement hussite, conservatoire musical de l'Europe, cœur immortel du carrefour de l'histoire dont le rythme a souvent donné l'impulsion aux grands événements de l'histoire mondiale.

Prague… Ville Dorée, Ville aux cent tours, baignant son front dans la Vltava…

Epithètes maintes et maintes fois reprises au cours des siècles tant dans les vers du poète que sous le pinceau de l'artiste… Epithètes toujours chères au cœur de ceux qui ont vu Prague, ne serait-ce qu'une fois.

En quoi réside donc cette attraction magique qui embue d'émotion et d'admiration l'œil du voyageur le plus blasé? D'où provient ce charme qui envoûte tous ceux qui, bien que connaissant les plus belles villes du monde, tombent amoureux de l'ensorcelante Prague dès qu'ils la voient?

Est-ce là l'effet du vertigineux tourbillon d'impressions qui vous assaillent devant tant de beautés jaillissantes comme de capiteuses fontaines hors de sources antiques, nourries par des siècles d'une effervescente vie politique et artistique?

Ou bien est-ce là le fait de ces mille aspects dont Prague se plaît à se parer, toujours aussi captivante malgré la funeste atteinte des ans qui, d'ailleurs ne l'a pas entravée dans sa marche et ne l'a pas empêchée de prendre place parmi les grandes villes modernes du monde contemporain?

Oui… mille aspects, mille visages splendides, taillés par les siècles comme une pierre précieuse… Combien d'entre eux, témoins muets de la naissance et de la croissance de la ville, qui détient fidèlement le trésor de ses souvenirs architecturaux et artistiques… Siècle après siècle, la Vltava murmure sa douce chanson entre les rives de Prague et Prague mire dans ses eaux un visage toujours changeant, toujours nouveau… Comment choisir et dire lequel est le plus beau?

Et pourtant… il en est un plus prenant encore que les autres, bien que les ans l'aient sillonné de rides profondes et que le cours trépidant et sauvage de la vie l'ait marqué de

l'empreinte du modernisme. C'est le plus vieux visage de Prague, „La mère des villes",
émouvant et cher comme le visage d'une mère où la vieillesse s'harmonise avec la grâce de
la jeunesse passée, fier de porter le sceau romantique des temps révolus et pourtant inspirant
aux nouvelles générations le sens de la beauté.

Eh bien! – regardons le les yeux dans les yeux, ce visage, si nous voulons connaître et
comprendre Prague. Descendons de la colline où s'ébaucha sa glorieuse et dramatique épopée, traversons ses jardins paradisiaques d'où nous parviendra peut-être, dans le chuchote-
ment des arbres séculaires, le lointain écho d'une tendre flûte pastorale...

Animons d'un pas sonore ces oasis de calme que sont les anciens palais de la noblesse,
égarons-nous sans crainte dans le labyrinthe des ruelles du quartier de Malá Strana et
arrêtons-nous de temps à autre pour jouir des spectacles enchanteurs que nous offrent ses
profondeurs béantes...

„L'Image de Prague" est le premier ouvrage de la nouvelle série ARTION. Il nous a
paru que l'on ne pouvait mieux fêter sa naissance qu'en l'inaugurant par un livre consacré
à l'antique beauté de la Ville aux cent tours.

Puisse cet ouvrage répandre bien au delà des frontières sa mission de beauté et trans-
mettre le salut amical d'une nation qui a mis tout son cœur, tout son amour et sa foi en
l'avenir et en sa gloire éternelle au service des mille et mille charmes de sa capitale...

Jiří Körber

ILLUSTRATIONS

les miracles de la nature font oublier le fardeau de la condition humaine et les souffrances d'ici bas.

17. La toute petite rivière ČERTOVKA, baignant depuis des siècles le pied des maisons de Malá Strana, anime et réanime sans trêve le paysage romantique d'une scène du passé. Arrêtées sont les roues des moulins qui ont moulu tant et tant de grain... arrêté est le cours du temps.

18. Mais un peu plus loin, la Vltava fredonne une nouvelle strophe de son éternelle chanson sur la marche sans retour des ans et des ans... le promeneur, lui, s'arrête sur la rive de l'île Kampa pour y goûter le charme irréel du pont qui se déroule, arche après arche, devant ses yeux, le plus vieux de Prague : le Pont Charles.

19. Quelques pas encore... et alors apparaît à nos yeux éblouis le panorama qui a ensorcelé à tout jamais ceux qui ont vu Prague, ne serait-ce qu'une fois : Le château royal et les palais des Hradčany, dominant la Vltava.

20. Le médiéval Pont Charles est, de plus, une véritable galerie de sculpture baroque tchèque. Les statues expressives qui ornent ses parapets sont en grande partie l'œuvre du célèbre maître Mathieu Braun et des deux Brokoff, elles datent du début du XVIIIème siècle.

21. La puissance captivante de la musique semble avoir marqué d'une trace indélébile la pierre du célèbre RUDOLFINUM, Maison des Artistes. Ancien siège du Parlement, le Rudolfinum a été rendu à son but initial et les festivals mondiaux du Printemps de Prague, dont les accents retentissent à l'ombre protectrice de la silhouette des Hradčany, célèbrent la gloire de la beauté et de la paix dans le monde.

22. Quittant le quartier de Malá Strana, nous pénétrerons non loin de là au cœur même de Prague : dans la Vieille Ville. Nous gravirons ces vieux escaliers, baignés d'un lumineux crépuscule, qui mènent à de calmes musées, détenteurs fidèles et sûrs des grands souvenirs historiques de la ville.

23. L'HÔTEL DE VILLE de la Vieille Ville, mémorial des époques les plus cruelles et les plus glorieuses de la nation tchèque, s'élève fièrement au carrefour même des siècles, là où se croisent les voies d'un passé infiniment lointain et les chemins de la vie moderne.

24. De l'Hôtel de Ville, s'offre une vue merveilleuse sur L'ÉGLISE DU TYN (datant des XIVème et XVème siècles), tant de fois immortalisée, non seulement sur la toile du peintre, mais encore sur les pages glorieuses de l'histoire du Mouvement hussite de Prague.

25. Éparses un peu partout dans la ville, les ruines des anciennes fortifications nous rappellent à chaque pas que Prague était jadis une place forte. Regardons tout particulièrement cette minuscule maison de la rue des Carmélites (Vieille Ville), tapie entre des immeubles modernes, qui a planté ses fondations dans les ruines de la plus vieille porte de Prague.

26. Inséparable du panorama des Hradčany et dominant de son imposante masse le quartier de Malá Strana, L'ÉGLISE SAINT NICOLAS, œuvre maîtresse de Kilian Ignace Dientzenhofer, est l'un des plus purs joyaux de l'art baroque tchèque.

27. De toutes ses pierres et de toute sa façade richement décorée, l'église Saint Nicolas semble être la gardienne du sanctuaire où dorment les rois tchèques de leur dernier sommeil : LA CATHEDRALE SAINT GUY du Château royal.

28. Ces dentelles de pierre qui parent la flèche de la Cathédrale Saint Guy sont, de par leur finesse arachnéenne, l'expression même du merveilleux épanouissement de l'ornementation gothique et leur perfection reste à tout jamais gravée dans la mémoire.

29. Les artistes qui ont succédé aux maîtres du gothique n'ont certes pas épargné leurs facultés créatrices et leur fantaisie en décorant la Vieille Ville, témoin en est la fontaine renaissance „NA MALÉM RYNEČKU".

30. Aujourd'hui, tout comme il y a cent ans, les fenêtres des maisons de Malá Strana sont grand'-ouvertes à la vie des petites rues si pittoresques et des places et c'est peut-être en hommage à sa joie et à sa gloire que les anciens propriétaires ont orné les portails et les corniches de leurs demeures de sculptures fort agréables à l'œil.

31. La richesse de forme et la fantaisie de l'art baroque ont permis dans une très large mesure aux bourgeois de l'ancienne Prague d'orner les frontons de leurs maisons, leur conférant ainsi une véritable personnalité et un cachet plein de charme.

32. Par contre, l'Eglise, comme si elle avait délibérément décidé de fermer ses portes à cette vie profane, élance la froide maçonnerie de ses tours majestueuses au plus haut des cieux, affirmant ainsi la force de son pouvoir. La tour de l'église dominicaine SAINT GILLES, rue de Hus, s'enorgueillit à juste titre de posséder la plus vieille cloche de Prague.

33. Quant à la noblesse du XVIème siècle, bien qu'ayant adhéré aux idéaux de la Renaissance, elle se sépare de la vie quotidienne et des gens du

commun et se mure en de pompeux palais. C'est de cette époque que date le PALAIS SCHWARZEN-BERG, dont la façade est richement ornée de peintures sur crépi.

34. Les escaliers, partie intégrante des vieux quartiers, conduisent souvent le promeneur, par un labyrinthe angoissant de ruelles, à des points de vue inattendus. Ainsi LES ESCALIERS DU CHATEAU (Zámecké schody) et la rue de Thun qui leur fait suite vous feront gravir la colline du Château par un chemin romantique à souhait.

35. Un rayon de soleil, semblable à un regard indiscret, éclaire l'espace d'un instant la grisaille de l'étroite RUELLE SASKA (derrière le Pont Charles) comme s'il voulait se persuader que tout est encore bien vivant en ces lieux ployants sous les ans.

36. Du haut de sa vaste esplanade, le Château royal nous fait don d'un merveilleux point de vue sur les vieux toits de tuiles de Malá Strana, noyés dans le vaporeux brouillard du point du jour ou bien émergeant du voile des crépuscules dorés.

37. De l'intérieur de l'église de la Vierge Marie sous la Chaîne on peut voir l'historique Place de Malte et la sculpture de St. Jean Baptiste, qui dans le temps formait le centre de la fontaine.

38. La lumière crue, implacable des projecteurs ne saurait trouver une faille dans l'immuable beauté des tours du Pont Charles. Bien au contraire, elle fait ressortir des profondeurs de la nuit les trésors architecturaux des siècles passés et les pare d'un charme encore plus ensorcelant.

39. La très remarquable et très précieuse TOUR NOIRE (Černá věž), bastion de la première fortification en pierre du Château, a gardé toute sa majesté malgré ses huit siècles d'âge et les flammes assassines des incendies.

40. Comme il est difficile de ne pas céder à la tentation de jeter un dernier coup d'œil sur tous ces hauts-lieux dont l'image est gravée au fond de notre cœur... Mais au dessus du Pont Charles, la nuit resserre peu à peu sa large étreinte et va doucement recouvrir le visage de Prague d'un voile constellé de rêves.

COUVERTURE (VERSO). Le monument du maître Jean Hus, devant l'église du Týn, incarne le souvenir et la gloire de Prague la Hussite qui, à la beauté, allie l'idéal élevé d'un peuple dont les bras accueillants sont toujours largement ouverts aux hommes de bonne volonté.

Jiří Körber

ImTheStory.com

Personalized Classic Books in many genre's

Unique gift for kids, partners, friends, colleagues

Customize:

- Character Names
- Upload your own front/back cover images (optional)
- Inscribe a personal message/dedication on the
  inside page (optional)

Customize many titles Including
- Alice in Wonderland
- Romeo and Juliet
- The Wizard of Oz
- A Christmas Carol
- Dracula
- Dr. Jekyll & Mr. Hyde
- And more...

CPSIA information can be obtained
at www.ICGtesting.com
Printed in the USA
LVOW13s1112240618
581731LV00026B/196/P